MW00899155

A new learning opportunity presents itself this week. Be bold and dive in, get emmersed, and enjoy yourself.

December/January 2020

VB

○ Monday 30

PRIORITIES

_____

_____

○ Tuesday 31

_____

_____

_____

_____

○ Wednesday 1

TO DO

_____

○ Thursday 2

_____

_____

_____

_____

○ Friday 3

_____

_____

_____

_____

○ Saturday 4 / Sunday 5

_____

_____

_____

Listen to your closest allies this week - a pooled opinion leads you to a new, healthier way of thinking.

January 2020

Week Number: 2

○ Monday 6

○ Tuesday 7

○ Wednesday 8

○ Thursday 9

○ Friday 10

○ Saturday 11 / Sunday 12

Something dear to you
will end this week.
The disappointment is
fleeting, it's important to
remember the good times.

January 2020

Week Number: 3

○ Monday 13

PRIORITIES

○ Tuesday 14

○ Wednesday 15

TO DO

○ Thursday 16

○ Friday 17

○ Saturday 18 / Sunday 19

A double-digit number ending in 8 is leading a path to some naughty indulgence. It won't pay out immediately, but it will be worth it.

January 2020

Week Number: 4

VB

○ Monday 20

PRIORITIES

○ Tuesday 21

○ Wednesday 22

TO DO

○ Thursday 23

○ Friday 24

○ Saturday 25 / Sunday 26

You seem to be channeling the spirit of a feline this week, as you're clinging defensively to routines and territory with claws out. Calm down a little.

January 2020

Week Number: 5

○ Monday 27

○ Tuesday 28

○ Wednesday 29

TO DO

○ Thursday 30

○ Friday 31

○ Saturday 1 / Sunday 2

It's like you've charged up with the magnetism of Ganymede this week. This kind of energy could move mountains (or just tidy a room or two).

February 2020

Week Number: 6

VȢ

○ Monday 3

○ Tuesday 4

○ Wednesday 5

TO DO

○ Thursday 6

○ Friday 7

○ Saturday 8 / Sunday 9

You're all claws and insecurities this week, and you're not a cat, so you need to cool off a little.

February 2020

Week Number: 7

○ Monday 10

PRIORITIES

○ Tuesday 11

○ Wednesday 12

TO DO

○ Thursday 13

○ Friday 14

○ Saturday 15 / Sunday 16

Brace for a little trouble in the next few days. Open your heart to a distant connection to relieve the stress.

February 2020

Week Number: 8

Ʋʒ

○ Monday 17

PRIORITIES

○ Tuesday 18

○ Wednesday 19

TO DO

○ Thursday 20

○ Friday 21

○ Saturday 22 / Sunday 23

Unhealthy choices bring you down this week, but a new business gives you a starting point to heal.

February 2020

Week Number: 9

VB

○ Monday 24

○ Tuesday 25

○ Wednesday 26

TO DO

○ Thursday 27

○ Friday 28

○ Saturday 29 / Sunday 1

That Taurus thinks they're so superior, and it's not just you that's getting ruffled by it. Choose between hurting them, and winning others over.

March 2020
Week Number: 10

○ Monday 2

PRIORITIES

_____
_____
_____
_____
_____

○ Tuesday 3

○ Wednesday 4

TO DO

_____
_____
_____
_____
_____

○ Thursday 5

○ Friday 6

○ Saturday 7 / Sunday 8

That big occasion coming up seems stressful to think about, but you're going to need to focus to find the one thing you forgot to prepare.

March 2020

VB

○ Monday 9

PRIORITIES

_____

_____

○ Tuesday 10

_____

_____

_____

_____

○ Wednesday 11

TO DO

_____

_____

○ Thursday 12

_____

_____

_____

_____

_____

○ Friday 13

_____

_____

_____

_____

○ Saturday 14 / Sunday 15

_____

_____

_____

When you feel down this week, ask yourself when the last time was you drank water. Chances are, a little hydration and self awareness will ease the pain.

March 2020

Week Number: 12

VB

○ Monday 16

○ Tuesday 17

○ Wednesday 18

○ Thursday 19

○ Friday 20

○ Saturday 21 / Sunday 22

You've said for months that you'd deal with it, and this is the week to do it. It will go well.

March 2020

○ Monday 23

PRIORITIES

○ Tuesday 24

○ Wednesday 25

TO DO

○ Thursday 26

○ Friday 27

○ Saturday 28 / Sunday 29

A little self-care is needed this week. Pamper yourself, spend a little money on you, and enjoy the power in you to make yourself happy.

March/April 2020

VB

○ Monday 30

_____

_____

○ Tuesday 31

_____

_____

_____

_____

○ Wednesday 1

TO DO

_____

○ Thursday 2

_____

_____

_____

_____

○ Friday 3

_____

_____

_____

_____

○ Saturday 4 / Sunday 5

_____

_____

_____

Sometimes decisions are not obvious. There's no harm in flipping a coin this week to decide.

April 2020

Week Number: 15

♑

○ Monday 6

○ Tuesday 7

○ Wednesday 8

TO DO

○ Thursday 9

○ Friday 10

○ Saturday 11 / Sunday 12

Listen to your alarm clock this week, it's trying to tell you about a fruitful opportunity.

April 2020

○ Monday 13

PRIORITIES

○ Tuesday 14

○ Wednesday 15

TO DO

○ Thursday 16

○ Friday 17

○ Saturday 18 / Sunday 19

Oh Leos, always seeking (and hogging) the limelight. One particular Leo close to you might be willing to share theirs if you ask nicely.

April 2020

Week Number: 17

♏

○ Monday 20

PRIORITIES
_____
_____
_____
_____
_____
_____

○ Tuesday 21

○ Wednesday 22

TO DO
_____
_____
_____
_____
_____

○ Thursday 23

_____
_____
_____
_____

○ Friday 24

_____
_____
_____
_____

○ Saturday 25 / Sunday 26

_____
_____
_____

Bad words will hurt your heart, but you will find strength from an unlikely source.

April 2020

Week Number: 18

♑

○ Monday 27

PRIORITIES

_____

_____

○ Tuesday 28

_____

_____

_____

_____

○ Wednesday 29

TO DO

_____

○ Thursday 30

_____

_____

_____

_____

○ Friday 1

_____

_____

_____

_____

○ Saturday 2 / Sunday 3

_____

_____

_____

Honey, you wouldn't treat
your friends like this, so
why are you doing this
to yourself? It's time
to apologize to your
inner self with a little
pampering.

May 2020

Week Number: 19

◯ Monday 4

PRIORITIES

◯ Tuesday 5

◯ Wednesday 6

TO DO

◯ Thursday 7

◯ Friday 8

◯ Saturday 9 / Sunday 10

Deep sadness is sometimes unavoidable - you have the power in you this week to help someone through a tough time.

May 2020

Week Number: 20

Vß

○ Monday 11

PRIORITIES

_____

_____

○ Tuesday 12

_____

_____

_____

_____

○ Wednesday 13

TO DO

_____

○ Thursday 14

_____

_____

_____

_____

○ Friday 15

_____

_____

_____

_____

○ Saturday 16 / Sunday 17

_____

_____

_____

You're going to feel a little sad when you check the forecast this week, but trust that this shift in systems is going to bring a positive shift in your life too.

May 2020

VB

○ Monday 18

PRIORITIES

○ Tuesday 19

○ Wednesday 20

TO DO

○ Thursday 21

○ Friday 22

○ Saturday 23 / Sunday 24

A long to-do list is hiding
an amazing opportunity.
Don't delay it any further.

May 2020

Week Number: 22

V3

○ Monday 25

PRIORITIES

○ Tuesday 26

○ Wednesday 27

TO DO

○ Thursday 28

○ Friday 29

○ Saturday 30 / Sunday 31

Your private space is feeling cluttered, and the work needed to clear it seems overwhelming. Start with something small, and give yourself rewards along the way.

June 2020

Week Number: 23

○ Monday 1

PRIORITIES

_____

_____

○ Tuesday 2

_____

_____

_____

○ Wednesday 3

TO DO

_____

○ Thursday 4

_____

_____

_____

_____

○ Friday 5

_____

_____

_____

○ Saturday 6 / Sunday 7

_____

_____

_____

A previously unclear message will make a lot more sense to you this week, and is an excellent starting point for something.

June 2020

Week Number: 24

○ Monday 8

PRIORITIES

_____

_____

○ Tuesday 9

_____

_____

_____

_____

○ Wednesday 10

TO DO

_____

_____

○ Thursday 11

_____

_____

_____

_____

○ Friday 12

_____

_____

_____

_____

○ Saturday 13 / Sunday 14

_____

_____

_____

Brace for a little shake-up in the next few days. Open your heart to a unlikely companion to relieve the worry.

June 2020

Week Number: 25

○ Monday 15

○ Tuesday 16

○ Wednesday 17

○ Thursday 18

○ Friday 19

○ Saturday 20 / Sunday 21

A piece of artwork speaks to you this week. You do not need to act right now, but soon it will be crucial.

June 2020

Week Number: 26

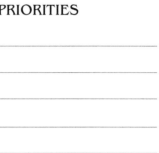

○ Monday 22

PRIORITIES

_____

_____

○ Tuesday 23

_____

_____

_____

_____

○ Wednesday 24

TO DO

_____

○ Thursday 25

_____

_____

_____

_____

○ Friday 26

_____

_____

_____

_____

○ Saturday 27 / Sunday 28

_____

_____

_____

A close friend needs your firm voice this week. Keep a level head for them, and you will inspire positive change.

June/July 2020

VB

○ Monday 29

PRIORITIES

_____

_____

○ Tuesday 30

_____

_____

_____

○ Wednesday 1

TO DO

_____

○ Thursday 2

_____

_____

_____

○ Friday 3

_____

_____

_____

○ Saturday 4 / Sunday 5

_____

_____

Spring cleaning gives you
the mental calmness you
have needed for months.
Prioritize it this week.

July 2020
Week Number: 28

V3

○ Monday 6

PRIORITIES

○ Tuesday 7

○ Wednesday 8

TO DO

○ Thursday 9

○ Friday 10

○ Saturday 11 / Sunday 12

Something you own too many of needs to be dealt with this week. Consider donating to charity or helping a friend in need.

July 2020

VƆ

○ Monday 13

PRIORITIES

_____

_____

○ Tuesday 14

_____

_____

_____

_____

○ Wednesday 15

TO DO

_____

○ Thursday 16

_____

_____

_____

_____

○ Friday 17

_____

_____

_____

_____

○ Saturday 18 / Sunday 19

_____

_____

_____

A big change results in hiccups in the next few days until a work colleague shows you how to get over it.

July 2020

Week Number: 30

○ Monday 20

PRIORITIES

○ Tuesday 21

○ Wednesday 22

TO DO

○ Thursday 23

○ Friday 24

○ Saturday 25 / Sunday 26

That Scorpio you know
is up to something.
While your fire is hot, be
cautious of their ability to
make steam.

July 2020

○ Monday 27

PRIORITIES

○ Tuesday 28

○ Wednesday 29

TO DO

○ Thursday 30

○ Friday 31

○ Saturday 1 / Sunday 2

You're feeling yourself slipping back into your old ways, thank goodness you noticed though. Now you can do something about it.

August 2020

Week Number: 32

VЗ

○ Monday 3

PRIORITIES

_____

_____

○ Tuesday 4

_____

_____

_____

○ Wednesday 5

TO DO

_____

○ Thursday 6

_____

_____

_____

○ Friday 7

_____

_____

_____

_____

○ Saturday 8 / Sunday 9

_____

_____

Make a list of all the things
troubling you this week
and let the gentle motion
of the Earth calm you
through them.

August 2020

Week Number: 33

♑

○ Monday 10

PRIORITIES
_____
_____
_____
_____
_____

○ Tuesday 11

○ Wednesday 12

TO DO
_____
_____
_____
_____

○ Thursday 13

_____
_____

○ Friday 14

_____
_____
_____
_____

○ Saturday 15 / Sunday 16

_____
_____
_____

There's an Aquarius that's pissing everyone off, and you could be a hero by telling them what everyone thinks. But there's a personal cost.

August 2020

Week Number: 34

VB

○ Monday 17

PRIORITIES

_____
_____
_____
_____

○ Tuesday 18

_____
_____

○ Wednesday 19

TO DO

_____
_____

○ Thursday 20

_____
_____
_____
_____

○ Friday 21

_____
_____
_____
_____

○ Saturday 22 / Sunday 23

_____
_____
_____

A glance outside a familiar
window will give you
information you needed
this week.

August 2020

Week Number: 35

VЗ

○ Monday 24

○ Tuesday 25

○ Wednesday 26

TO DO

○ Thursday 27

○ Friday 28

○ Saturday 29 / Sunday 30

Get ready for an exciting visitor, they will bring with them a new hobby that you will love.

August/September 2020

Week Number: 36

VЗ

○ Monday 31

PRIORITIES

_____

_____

_____

_____

○ Tuesday 1

○ Wednesday 2

TO DO

_____

_____

_____

○ Thursday 3

_____

_____

_____

_____

○ Friday 4

_____

_____

_____

○ Saturday 5 / Sunday 6

_____

_____

_____

A life colleague feels a
little forgotten this week,
and you have a special
flare for cheering them up,
so go work it.

September 2020

Week Number: 37

VS

○ Monday 7

PRIORITIES

○ Tuesday 8

○ Wednesday 9

TO DO

○ Thursday 10

○ Friday 11

○ Saturday 12 / Sunday 13

Listen for someone with a sexy rasp this week. They have some neat introductions for you.

September 2020

Week Number: 38

Vߺ
<!-- zodiac symbol (Capricorn) -->

○ Monday 14

PRIORITIES

_____

_____

○ Tuesday 15

_____

_____

_____

○ Wednesday 16

TO DO

_____

○ Thursday 17

_____

_____

_____

_____

○ Friday 18

_____

_____

_____

_____

○ Saturday 19 / Sunday 20

_____

_____

_____

A very guarded Taurus is
questioning you right now.
Back up your claims with
proof though and they'll
be forced to believe you.

September 2020

○ Monday 21

PRIORITIES

○ Tuesday 22

○ Wednesday 23

TO DO

○ Thursday 24

○ Friday 25

○ Saturday 26 / Sunday 27

Careful now, you're appearing a little pompous about something you received over the weekend. Cool it now and you can save face.

September 2020

Week Number: 40

○ Monday 28

PRIORITIES

_____

○ Tuesday 29

_____

_____

○ Wednesday 30

TO DO

_____

○ Thursday 1

_____

_____

○ Friday 2

_____

_____

○ Saturday 3 / Sunday 4

_____

_____

A burst of energy allows you to get sometime rather tough done - keep the momentum going to achieve even greater things.

October 2020

Week Number: 41

♑

○ Monday 5

PRIORITIES

_____

_____

○ Tuesday 6

_____

_____

_____

○ Wednesday 7

TO DO

_____

_____

○ Thursday 8

_____

_____

_____

○ Friday 9

_____

_____

_____

_____

○ Saturday 10 / Sunday 11

_____

_____

_____

A new food is the key to bringing together a friendship that you've been chasing for a while, but only for this week, so act fast.

October 2020

Week Number: 42

♑

○ Monday 12

○ Tuesday 13

○ Wednesday 14

TO DO

○ Thursday 15

○ Friday 16

○ Saturday 17 / Sunday 18

A deep voice over the telephone is just the tonic you need. You will need to initiate the call though.

October 2020

Week Number: 43

○ Monday 19

PRIORITIES

_____

_____

○ Tuesday 20

_____

_____

_____

○ Wednesday 21

TO DO

_____

_____

○ Thursday 22

_____

_____

_____

_____

○ Friday 23

_____

_____

_____

○ Saturday 24 / Sunday 25

_____

_____

_____

If the opportunity arises to gamble on something this week, go all in, but don't forget to hydrate first!

October 2020

Week Number: 44

○ Monday 26

PRIORITIES

○ Tuesday 27

○ Wednesday 28

TO DO

○ Thursday 29

○ Friday 30

○ Saturday 31 / Sunday 1

Money will force you to make a tough decision this week. It is important to think wisely about the decision.

November 2020

Week Number: 45

VB

○ Monday 2

○ Tuesday 3

○ Wednesday 4

TO DO

○ Thursday 5

○ Friday 6

○ Saturday 7 / Sunday 8

When you neglect to water your life's houseplants, they take a little of your energy with them. It's a 5 minute task, go do it!

November 2020

V3

○ Monday 9

PRIORITIES

○ Tuesday 10

○ Wednesday 11

TO DO

○ Thursday 12

○ Friday 13

○ Saturday 14 / Sunday 15

Keep your friends close this week - the hivemind has some solid advice for you to improve your mental health.

November 2020

Week Number: 47

VƷ

○ Monday 16

PRIORITIES
_____
_____
_____
_____
_____

○ Tuesday 17

○ Wednesday 18

TO DO
_____
_____
_____

○ Thursday 19

_____
_____

○ Friday 20

_____
_____
_____
_____

○ Saturday 21 / Sunday 22

_____
_____

You're going to get chatting to someone new, and feel the urge to follow them somewhere. It's a risk for sure, so take precautions!

November 2020

Week Number: 48

VB

○ Monday 23

PRIORITIES

○ Tuesday 24

○ Wednesday 25

TO DO

○ Thursday 26

○ Friday 27

○ Saturday 28 / Sunday 29

You're tempted to assume you read that text wrong, but no, they really are mad at you. No, it's not fair, but you might have to swallow this one down.

November/December 2020

Week Number: 49

VB

○ Monday 30

○ Tuesday 1

○ Wednesday 2

TO DO

○ Thursday 3

○ Friday 4

○ Saturday 5 / Sunday 6

One of your biggest challenges is how rude you can be. Work on it this week for a potentially lucrative introduction.

December 2020

○ Monday 7

PRIORITIES

○ Tuesday 8

○ Wednesday 9

TO DO

○ Thursday 10

○ Friday 11

○ Saturday 12 / Sunday 13

An Aries with piercing eyes has the ability to lift your spirit this week. Engage them in a conversation about passions.

December 2020

Week Number: 51

♑

○ Monday 14

PRIORITIES

_____

_____

○ Tuesday 15

_____

_____

_____

○ Wednesday 16

TO DO

_____

○ Thursday 17

_____

_____

_____

○ Friday 18

_____

_____

_____

_____

○ Saturday 19 / Sunday 20

_____

_____

_____

A simple daily routine change will take you out of your comfort zone this week. Enjoy the diversion, it's along a scenic route.

December 2020

○ Monday 21

PRIORITIES

_____

_____

○ Tuesday 22

_____

_____

_____

_____

○ Wednesday 23

TO DO

_____

○ Thursday 24

_____

_____

_____

_____

○ Friday 25

_____

_____

_____

_____

○ Saturday 26 / Sunday 27

_____

_____

_____

_____

A familiar song carries a good message that will help you deal with some annoyances this week.

December 2020

Week Number: 53

♑

○ Monday 28

PRIORITIES

_____

_____

○ Tuesday 29

_____

_____

_____

○ Wednesday 30

TO DO

_____

_____

○ Thursday 31

_____

_____

_____

_____

○ Friday 1

_____

_____

_____

_____

○ Saturday 2 / Sunday 3

_____

_____

_____

CPSIA information can be obtained
at www.ICGtesting.com
Printed in the USA
LVHW082207231219
641548LV00018B/1305/P